Geography Starts

MOUNTAINS

Andy Owen
and
Miranda Ashwell

Heinemann Interactive Library
Des Plaines, Illinois

Designed by Susan Clarke
Illustrations by Oxford Illustrators (maps pp.23, 25, 27) and Hardlines (pp.5, 12)
Printed in Hong Kong

02 01 00 99
10 9 8 7 6 5 4 3 2

Library of Congress Cataloging-in-Publication Data
Owen, Andy, 1961-
    Mountains / Andy Owen and Miranda Ashwell.
      p.   cm. — (Geography starts)
    Includes bibliographical references and index.
    Summary: An introduction to the types and characteristics of mountains, including volcanoes and glaciers, and the disastrous effects on them of landslides and avalanches.
    ISBN 1-57572-607-6 (lib. bdg.)
    1. Mountains—Juvenile literature. [1. Mountains.] I. Ashwell, Miranda, 1957- . II. Title. III. Series: Owen, Andy, 1961- Geography starts.
GB512.094   1998
551.43'2—dc21   97-34420
                                        CIP
                                        AC

Acknowledgments
The Publishers would like to thank the following for permission to reproduce photographs:
Aerofilms, p.15; BBC/David Noton, p.17; Bruce Coleman Ltd, p.4 (Mr Jules Cowan), p.6 (Steven C. Kaufman), p.16 (C.C. Lockwood), p.19 (Dieter & Mary Plage); Environmental Images/Colin Cummings, p.20; Hutchinson, p.8 (Jeremy Horner), p.9 (Eric Lawrie); Images Colour Library, p.21; Mountain Camera/John Cleare, p.13; Nottingham Trent University/Tony Waltham, p.18; Robert Harding Picture Library, p.22; Royal Geographical Society, p.28; Sealand Aerial Photography, pp.24, 26; Still Pictures, p.11 (Georges Lopez), p.14 (Alan Watson); Tony Stone, p.10 (Ernest Braun), p.7 (Paul Chesley), p.29 (Dennis Oda)

Cover photograph: Robert Harding Picture Library

Our thanks to Betty Root for her comments in the preparation of this book.

Every effort has been made to contact copyright holders of any material reproduced in this book. Any omissions will be rectified in subsequent printings if notice is given to the Publisher.

Some words are shown in bold, like this. You can find out what they mean by looking in the glossary.

Contents

Making Mountains 4

Volcano 6

Sleeping Volcanoes 8

Parts of a Mountain 10

Going Up 12

Ice on the Mountain 14

Mountain Water 16

Desert Mountains 18

Falling Mountains 20

Mountain Map 1 22

Mountain Map 2 24

Mountain Map 3 26

Amazing Facts 28

Glossary 30

More Books to Read 31

Index 32

Making Mountains

Mountains are huge chunks of rock that rise above the earth. Some mountains began as **layers** of rock under the sea.

As the earth moved, the layers were pushed up and out of the sea.

Sand and mud fell to the bottom of the sea.

60 million years ago

The layers of mud turned to rock.

40 million years ago

The layers were pushed up and the sea got smaller.

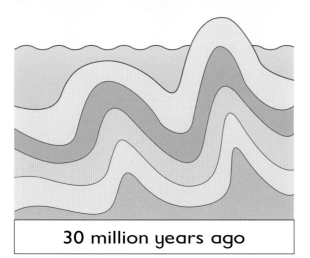

30 million years ago

The rock was pushed into **jagged** shapes above the sea.

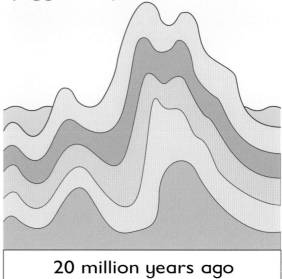

20 million years ago

Volcano

A **volcano** is a mountain that is still being made. When a volcano **erupts,** it blasts ash high into the sky.

Ash clouds can float very far and block out sunlight.

red hot lava

Rocks inside the volcano are so hot that
they melt. Melted rock is called lava. Lava is
thrown out of the volcano when it erupts.

Sleeping Volcanoes

When a **volcano erupts** it leaves a round hole called a crater. The crater can fill with water and make a lake.

a lake at the top of a volcano

8

This volcano has not erupted for a
long time. Snow covers the cold rocks.

Some volcanoes are quiet for a long time.
We say the volcano is dormant, or has
been sleeping. Then it may suddenly erupt.

Parts of a Mountain

The foothills are the lowest part of a mountain. Soil covers the rocks so many plants grow here.

Some people plant crops in the foothills.

steep slopes at the top

The top of the mountain is called
the summit. The summit is often
bare rocks with no soil or plants.

Going Up

The summit is the coldest part.
There is often snow and ice.

the snow line

Here it is still cold, but
there is no snow and ice.

The foothills are the
warmest part of the
mountain.

The higher up the mountain,
the colder it gets.

Some climbers must bring **oxygen** to help them breathe.

The air has less oxygen towards the top of a tall mountain. This makes breathing very hard.

Ice on the Mountain

Glaciers are large fields of ice. It takes thousands of years for a glacier to move down a mountain. As it moves, it cuts into the rocks.

The **jagged** rocks above this glacier were cut by ice.

This valley was made by a glacier thousands of years ago.

A **valley** is made when the glacier melts. The steep sides and flat bottom of the valley were made by the moving glacier.

Mountain Water

As water flows down the mountain, it makes a deep cut in the rock called a gorge. It takes thousands of years for a river to make a gorge.

The Grand Canyon in Arizona is one mile (1.6 kilometers) deep.

Waterfalls cut into the mountain.

Some steep mountain cliffs are cut by falling water. The mountain is slowly worn down by the moving water.

Desert Mountains

Rocks are warmed by the sun in the day. They cool down at night. This makes the rock crack and break off in **layers**.

When layers break off, they often make interesting patterns.

These mountains are
slowly crumbling.

Some mountains in dry places have flat tops
and steep cliffs. In this desert, huge pieces of
rock stick out of the desert, like fingers.

Falling Mountains

Large pieces of rock can suddenly break off the mountain side. The rocks tumble and slide down. This is called a landslide.

Landslides can block roads and trap people.

Snow can suddenly fall down steep mountain slopes. This is called an avalanche. An avalanche grows bigger as it tumbles down the mountain.

Avalanches will crush anything in their way.

Mountain Map 1

These mountains rise high above the sea. You cannot tell how high a mountain is by looking at a photograph.

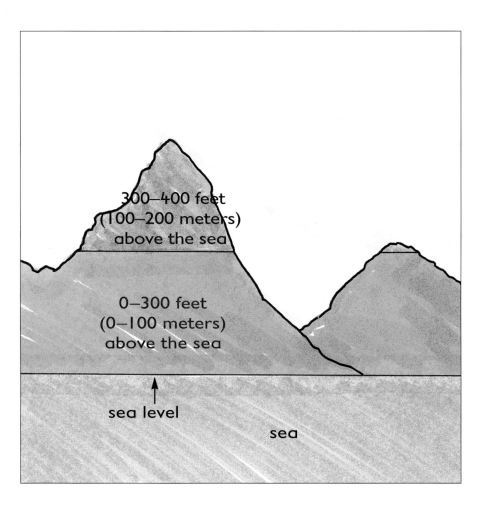

300–400 feet
(100–200 meters)
above the sea

0–300 feet
(0–100 meters)
above the sea

sea level

sea

The colors on this picture show how high the mountains are above the sea.

Mountain Map 2

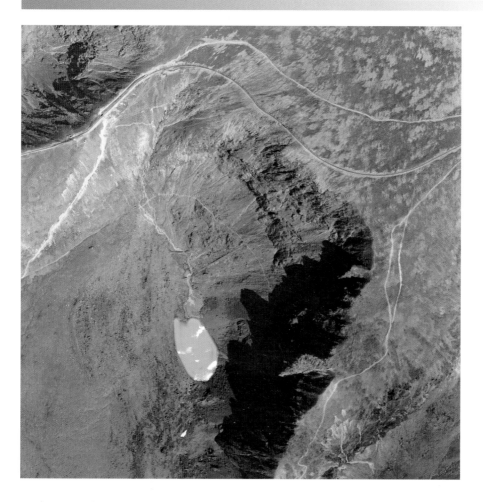

This photo shows a part of a mountain. It was taken from an airplane. You can see a road leading up to the summit. There is a small lake at the bottom of a steep slope.

Key

▨	land between 1,300–2,000 feet (400–600 meters) high
▨	land between 600–1,300 feet (200–400 meters) high
▨	lake
≈	steep, rocky slopes
≈	road

The purple color shows the highest part of the mountain. The steep, rocky slopes are shown with short black lines. Brown shows the lowest part where there is a lake.

Mountain Map 3

This photo shows another part of the same mountain. The **valley** is at the bottom of the photo. There is a river and a road in the valley.

Key		
▨	land between 1,300–2,000 feet (400–600 meters) high
▢	land between 600–1,300 feet (200–400 meters) high
▢	river
≋	steep rocky slopes
∿	road

Lines are used to show the road and the river. This map makes it easy to see the fields in the valley.

Amazing Facts

Mount Everest is the highest mountain on land. The first people to climb Everest were Edmund Hillary and Tenzing Norgay in 1953.

The top of Everest is 29,028 feet (8,848 meters) above the sea.

The largest **volcano** in the world is Mauna Loa on the island of Hawaii. It once **erupted** for one and a half years.

Rivers of lava can flow as fast as 550 feet (168 meters) per second.

Glossary

erupts   when hot rocks burst out of a volcano

jagged   having sharp points or edges

layers   thicknesses or levels

oxygen   gas that people, animals, and plants need to live

valley   low land between hills

volcano   opening in the earth where lava comes out, often making a mountain

More Books to Read

Baker, Susan. *First Look at Mountains*. Milwaukee: Gareth Stevens, 1991.

Barrett, Norman S. *Mountains*. New York: Franklin Watts, 1991.

Curran, Eileen. *Mountains and Volcanoes*. Mahwah, NJ: Troll Communications, 1985.

Lye, Keith. *Mountains*. Austin, Tex: Raintree Steck-Vaughn, 1992.

Stone, Lynn. *Mountains*. Danbury, Conn: Children's Press, 1983.

Zoehfeld, Kathleen. *How Mountains are Made*. New York: HarperCollins, 1995.

Index

avalanche 21

crater 8

erupt 6, 8, 29

glacier 14, 15

gorge 16

lake 8, 24, 25

landslide 20

lava 7, 29

layers 4, 18

maps 23, 25, 27

summit 11

valley 15, 26, 27

volcano 6, 7, 8, 9, 29

waterfalls 17